From Freemasonry to Christ

For practising or non-practising Freemasons
throughout the world who would,
if challenged, profess to be Christians.

by
Terry C Young

published in association with
MOORLEY'S Print & Publishing

ISBN 978-086071-608-2

First Published October 1995
2nd Revised Edition June 2007

Cover Concept: Caroline Jordan
                                    The Studio
                                    Upton
                                    Nottinghamshire

Printing & Trade Distribution by

MOORLEY'S Print & Publishing

23 Park Rd., Ilkeston, Derbys DE7 5DA
⤳⊙   Tel/Fax: (0115) 932 0643   ⊂✕

Acknowledgements

Firstly I would like to thank the following church members who, like myself, are former Freemasons and who very kindly took time to read and comment on my original script. My thanks therefore go to Anthony Hustwayte, Nigel Catley, Leslie Stone and the late John Stone.

My sincere thanks also to Caroline Jordan for her artistic help in designing the cover and to Anthony Hustwayte for his invaluable help in the layout and provision of the final text for the printers.

Finally a sincere thank you to my wife Penny for her patience in reading, correcting and typing my various drafts.

INTRODUCTION

I am writing this as a former Freemason for 22 years and now a practising Christian, to express the belief that Freemasonry is not compatible with Christianity. It does not set out to provide a detailed explanation of the reasons why, but is meant to give the main reasons, and it is hoped that it will lead to further reading and the ultimate renouncing of all membership in Freemasonry.

At the age of 21 and at the special request of my father, who was not then a Freemason, I asked a friend of his if I could become a Freemason. Within weeks I was admitted as an Entered Apprentice, and subsequently progressed to the full title of a Master Mason. Thereafter I diligently and enthusiastically studied the teachings and progressed through the offices to become Worshipful Master and a Past Master of the Lodge of which I was a member in London. In later years I joined the "Royal Arch" Chapter and it was whilst I was in office that I renounced all my associations with Freemasonry.

The sad thing to me is that throughout all my 22 years in membership I professed to be a Christian and believed I was a member of a good Christian organisation supported by members of the Royal Family, Church clergy and church-going friends of my own.

The turning point came when I realised that Christianity and being a Christian was more than just being a church-goer or a member of a church and a respected member of the community. To be a Christian is to know Jesus Christ as a personal friend and His code of conduct for our daily living. I turned to Jesus Christ in prayer, repenting of my sins and asking Him to reveal more of Himself to me so that I could follow His code of conduct. And then gradually over a period of some 18 months He showed me with the help of other Christians that the code of practice of Freemasonry was not consistent with the Christian code of conduct.

Consequently I resigned my membership and disposed of all my regalia, ritual books and membership certificates.

Some 14 years on from that time I know without any doubt that I was absolutely right to renounce Freemasonry as a Christian believing in Jesus Christ and His teachings.

I believe that there are many men, and to a lesser extent women, all over the world who profess to be Christians, who like myself have been members of Freemasonry for a number of years and have been persuaded into believing that Freemasonry is a very good and honourable institution.

Deception

In actual fact, Freemasonry is a subversive, anti-Christian movement which leaves out all references to Jesus Christ and forbids mention of His name. It only refers to a god who is the Great Architect of the Universe - GATU. Further study and participation in the ritual reveals that this GATU is in fact the devil.

Deception is the ruling principle of Freemasonry for in it is a skilful uniting of idolatry and paganism with Christian terms. From a Christian standpoint the Masonic ritual and ceremonies are a parody of Christianity. Candidates "in a state of darkness" have their blindfolds removed as a sign that they have now received the light "from above" and are ready to be admitted to the mysteries and privileges of Freemasonry. These will be obtained "with God's help", the implication being that, through practising Freemasonry, the initiate is setting out on a path of progressive enlightenment, and that by acquiring further hidden knowledge, continuing good conduct and attending Masonic ceremonies, he will draw closer to God. To a Christian, Jesus Christ is "the way" to God; it is His code of conduct that is the key to life for everyone. Moreover, it is Jesus Christ Himself who is the source of all truth and enlightenment, which he freely bestows on all His followers by His Holy Spirit.

The Name of God

Much of this deception is not revealed until a Freemason progresses into higher degrees, usually some years later, by which time members can see nothing morally wrong with the movement - which was the case with myself.

For example, the third degree ceremony of a Master Mason is incomplete and talks of a lost secret which is the name of God. This lost name is revealed in "Royal Arch" Chapter, a higher degree to which a Freemason (i.e. a Master Mason) can seek to become a member. As I write this in April 2007, the lost name is revealed as Jehovah. The latter is a transliteration of the Hebrew tetragram for the name of the one true God. Whereas it would appear that the use of the word Jehovah implies a belief in God, the deception is the use of the word in a ritual where throughout there is a skilful unity of idolatry and paganism with Christian terms. To explain further, before the use of the word Jehovah, the name was (until 1989) described as JAHBULON:

JAH being the Hebrew word in the Old Testament for God or Jehovah;

BUL meaning Baal, the Babylonian god;

ON meaning Osiris, the Egyptian god.

After February 1989, following strong pressure as a result of media revelation, United Grand Lodge changed the revealed name to JHVH. This tetragram stood for the Hebrew God whose name becomes anglicised as Jehovah, a name familiar to all Jews and Christians.

It is apparent that over a period of years, some effort has been made to soften the deception which would not be so obvious to newer members in Freemasonry.   Freemasons, however, are still told not to reveal or utter the name of Jehovah to anyone in the world, except in the company of at least two other recognised Master Masons.   The fact that a Freemason who professes to be a Christian is not allowed to reveal the name of Jehovah, is of course contrary to the code of conduct of a Christian.

God the Father

How can it be said that Freemasonry is compatible with Christianity when it invites men and women from all over the world to be members, some of whom are members of other faiths which do not recognise the divinity of Jesus Christ as the Son of God? When I went for my interview to join Freemasonry as a young man of 21, I was asked the question "Do you believe in God?" The question now asked is, "Do you believe in a supreme being?" The latter is much more suited to members of different faiths, but to a Christian, it is more appropriate to be asked if you believe in God the Father, Son (Jesus Christ) and Holy Spirit because the demons also believe in one God and tremble (according to James 2: 19). When a Christian is asked if they believe, the response should be clearly understood to be through a belief in the person of Jesus Christ, who came to reveal the Father to us. (John 14:6-7; 5:21-23; 8:19).

It is strictly forbidden to talk about Christianity when Freemasons meet together: this is because the god of Freemasonry is not the God, the Father of our Lord Jesus Christ, but can be anything one conceives him to be. This Masonic concept is "deism" and is the reason for labelling the one true God as the GATU. If Christians obey this Masonic rule they are surely not obeying Jesus when He commanded His followers to go into all the world and speak to all people about the Good News of the Gospel of Jesus Christ, who died for the forgiveness of sins that they might be reconciled to God and draw near to Him through His mercy and not through their striving to achieve salvation by good deeds. Freemasonry reduces salvation to a code of conduct in moral living without the emphasis on sin and grace, repentance and forgiveness to be found through Jesus Christ.

The Occult

Behind Masonic symbolism lies an occult significance of which most Freemasons who do not go beyond the first level of a Master Mason are unaware.

The symbols are ancient ones originating in Eastern mysticism and used in witchcraft and mystery religions; they are the means through which the devil receives worship. Ancient mystery religions once posed a great threat to early Christianity, constituting as they did a widespread system of corruption and idolatry, and promising initiates salvation through access to secret knowledge. Clearly from the Bible, any occult association is abhorrent to God and is to be avoided by a Christian.

A very serious side of being involved in occult teaching is that it can open the door in a person's life and in the life of his family, to demonic activity, which can manifest itself through their behaviour (e.g. a bad temper), through health or relationship problems. It is also impossible to reconcile Freemasonry with Christianity because of the "solemn obligations" and numerous oaths which candidates to any level of Freemasonry have to comply with under the threat of the most hideous penalties if they break them. If the barbaric oaths are to be taken seriously, then they constitute a murder pact; if not, then they occasion the misuse of the word Jehovah. Either way, agreeing to these oaths is opposed to the Christian's code of conduct. The Bible is very clear on the matter of oaths. (Matthew 5:34-37)

Finally, let the Encyclopaedia of Freemasonry, prepared by one of the greatest Masonic authors, speak for itself: "The religion of Freemasonry is not Christianity". (page 618)

If it were a Christian institution, adherents of other faiths could not be members. But the real question is: Is the god of Freemasonry the true God, or is he a false god? The answer depends without doubt on the Freemason's attitude towards Jesus Christ. The Father God of Christianity is unique; only the Judaeo-Christian faith has a God who provides a Saviour and who is present in His people by His Holy Spirit. As stated earlier, the teaching of Freemasonry avoids any reference to Jesus Christ in all the 33 levels of Freemasonry. A Christian life is one of allegiance to Him, for without Him we live in darkness and are liable to deception. Jesus said that He is the light of the world, and that whoever follows Him will not live in darkness but will have the light of life. (John 8:12)

Your response

If you are a Freemason, believe yourself to be a Christian and you feel these words have spoken to you, I believe that Jesus Christ is ready to begin to set you free from the harmful influence of Freemasonry.

May I offer a few words of suggestion and at the same time a few words of warning? As soon as possible seek out a Christian who is filled with the power of the Holy Spirit, who will pray with you to be completely and wholly released from any Masonic influence in your life. The word of warning is: be careful who you choose to pray for you because there are many church leaders of various denominations who are themselves Freemasons. Particularly be careful if you are a member of the Anglican Church where many of the clergy are themselves members.

As you take this step of obedience and faith in Jesus Christ be prepared for Him to start to do some amazing things in your life.

In a last action, remember to dispose of your

Masonic regalia, ritual books and membership certificate. It is important that you do not keep anything as a memento, but completely dissociate yourself from its influence.

And finally, may the Father of our Lord Jesus Christ bless you and keep you in His peace now and always. Amen.

*Terry Young lives in Southwell, Nottinghamshire,
where he is an active member of a local church.*

For further reading

John Lawrence: Freemasonry - A Religion?
(Kingsway Publications, Eastbourne, East
Sussex; 1987)

E. M. Storms: Should a Christian be a Mason?
(New Puritan Library, Fletcher, N.C., USA; 1980

Ian Gordon: The Craft and the Cross (The
Branch Press, Norwich ISBN 0-9528865-0-2)

David W. M. Vaughan: The Diary of a Freed
Mason (Sovereign World Ltd, PO Box 17,
Chichester PO20 6RY ISBN 1-85240-006-4)

The Internet or any good Christian Bookshop
should be able to provide more detailed
information.

Further copies of this booklet may be obtained
from your local Christian Bookshop or direct
from:

MOORLEY'S Print & Publishing
23 Park Rd., Ilkeston,
Derbys DE7 5DA
Tel/Fax: (0115) 932 0643
Email: sales@moorleys.co.uk